Homebody

AF669480

Anneliese Unger

BookLeaf
Publishing

Homebody © 2022 Anneliese Unger

All rights reserved.

No part of this publication may be reproduced, stored in a retrieval system, or transmitted, in any form or by any means, electronic, mechanical, photocopying, recording or otherwise, without the prior written permission of the presenters.

Anneliese Unger asserts the moral right to be identified as author of this work.

Presentation by *BookLeaf Publishing*

Web: www.bookleafpub.com

E-mail: info@bookleafpub.com

ISBN: 9789357696562

First edition 2022

DEDICATION

To A.W.C.T

Let the un-P.C adventures continue!

ACKNOWLEDGEMENT

I acknowledge this country and it's peoples as one nation, it's unity a work in progress that I fully support.

PREFACE

A jump into the swirling murkiness of my memories over a lifetime that is still being played out

Exit

A moan,
To
Chill my blood?
Nay to welcome with tired ecstasy.
This mewling parcel, slimy and bloated
streaks of red, slick and deformed
Unfurling, whimpering
Searching for the node, glorious
Weeping, milk and mother as one
Suckling and sated.
The grip of both, united.
And then the cut, the detriment of neither.
Independence? Yes, but symbolic; for our future,
when mine and hers becomes.

Hungry

The spray.
My face
My eyes
Open close, peekaboo.
Like white satin
Sweet silky
Comforting
Slipping into slumber, kneading.
Wail. Absence. Hiccup. Grunt. Snort. Wail.
Louder. LOUDER.
SCREECH.
Suckle. Soft. Warm. Squeeze. Ahhh bliss.
Massage. Knead. Suckle. Bite?
Whisked away. FAST.

Make a stand

Pull pull PULL.
Up up up and not quite away.
Look at that shiny, clanking, beeping, buzz.
Crash. Ok that is DOWN.
Pull. Pull. PULL.
Bing -BONG -Bam- Clank- BOiiiiiNG
Giggle. Coo. GRAB.
Step, step, crash!!
Waaaaaaaaaaaaaaaa

Twinkle tinkle I’m a little star

Squish squash squelch.
Soggy, smelly, hanging low.
Low rider.
Poke. Sniff. Look. Grimace.
Wash, wipe, dust.
Raspbeeeeeeerrrrrrrryyyyyyyy belly.
Tinkle tinkle tinkle.
"Oh Charlie!"
Wipe. Wipe. Wipe. Wipe.
Quick fast...
Crinkle, slap, tab both sides.
Smiles.

Good arm

Click click, tighten.
Airplane spoon.
Turn away. Look away. Mouth bubbles.
Smoosh. Squish. Splodge. Slap. Smush.
DROP.
Oooooooooh!
DROP. DROP. DROP.
Up. Up. Up. UP AGAIN!!!!
Flick. Ping. Throw. Drop. Drop. DROP
Up again.
Hmmmmmmmmmmmmm

Drop.

Swimming lessons

Splash. Splash. Splosh, splosh PANIC!
Breathe.
Water in. Choke. Gurgle. Cough.
Slap. Slap. Slap.
Head under. Don't breathe. Dizzy. Breathe.
Water in. Choke. Gurgle. Cough.
Slap. Slap. SLAP.
Head under. Don't breathe.
Kick. Kick. Kick. Up. Up. Up. Breathe.
Giggles. Laughter. Splash. Giggle.
Head under. Kick. Kick. Kick up.
Breathe.
GRIN.

Helmet on

Push. Push. Pedal pedal.
Feet spindles, around around, as up and down up and down.
Forwards ever forwards. Faster faster. Around.
Knees bobbing up and down. Jackhammer pace.
Jugjugjugjugjuggggggghhhhh.

Wheels off. Crank crank.
Pat on the back.
"You've got this Charlie"
Push. Pedal pedal. Jackhamm........Crunch. Scrape.

Blue metal. Pick. Pick. Wipe.
Legs AND conk; leaky bits.
Lots of leaky bits. Blurry.
Jackhammer legs. Push. Pedal. Pedal. Pe.... Crunch.

Blue metal. Pick. Pick. Wipe. No leaks.
Push. Jackhammer legs. Pedal. Pedal.
STEER. Pedal. Steer. Pedal. Vooommmmm VOOM.
Cheering. Sore knees. Pedal. Pedal. Pride.

Birthdays

Crazy grins and smiles.
Bursts of round colour, some bursting
Bang! Bang! Rubber confetti flying. Squeals of excite
and ancient ones groaning.
People roaming, holding, passing, grabbing
Wet cheeks.
A circle. Soprano voices and dowdy ones.
Chanting all.
Happy birthday.
Melting, icing; candles too.
Holding puff, thinking, wishing.
Exploding breath onto cream sponge and Spider-Man
blue.
Sticky fingers, belly crawling, the thirst.
Scrunch of paper flying.
Tip. Tear. Tears.
The old ones not mine. Snap snap. Lots of cheese,
none for eating.
Zoom ....cars, wait ...helicopter, no! water gun, wait
-Rip the wrap. Don't wrap the rip
Small mountains, paper mountains, toy mountains,
toy cars driving paper mountains wishing of camping
tented mountains

Summer clamshells

Blue.
Hard plastic.
Snaking green hose, hot water gushing to cool.
Sprinkle rainbows, wet trampolines, a bounce and a squelch! Wet feet, dripping bangs, stretched rashies.
Water bombs spraying rainbow SLAP confetti through the buffalo, bindis in the feet. Yelp, squelch. Grass rash, itch itch, the burn of the mini cuts fire.
Super soaker on the hip. Run, skid, dip, squirt. Howling and soggy, refill time. Run on tiptoes across the road, tar sticking to soles, blisters blossoming. Walk on the white, walk on the wet, quick!....onto the grass to rest. Back on the bitumen, back on the burn. Melting.
Icecream truck song chiming in the culdesac. Running, jingling, pockets clinking. Choc dip or sprinkle puddle, choose your sticky handed poison. White splats, cone droppings follow you; drip drop splat

Surfs Yalling-UP

Combi van. Wafting smells. The brown bean of awakening on awakening. Slurped from soggy paper vessels, the running burn, the warm chest, the fire lighting from my core, zapping up the jumper lead to my consciousness. Awake. Alert. Alarm.
Into the cold, the salty wet. Sloshing, cool vines of liquid snaking up my legs, belly wincing, cool heat making my shoulders tense. The pip under my arm, warm honey tones wafting up. Waxing lyrical?, nay waxing boards. Pulling up and fowards, belly supple and strong, arms digging, rhythmical. Over. Through. Up and over. Salty eyes. Turning my back to the blue. Waiting for the height; to slip in and surf that foamy rush back. A race; Back to the warm. Back to the warm, awaiting again the bean cup of liquid consciousness.

Strawberry smash

Rows and rows and rows. But no oars to be
seen.
Red green red green red green.
Black plastic in lines like obedient soldiers
marching to war-
Against bugs, cabbage moth, snails and
homeless snails;
Slugs they be.
War it is, an onslaught of green poison raining
down, pellets spraying left and right. Casualties
many. Frothing from the mouth or foot?
Picking them off slowly now, one by one.
Sneaky like. Red running down my arms. The
fields awash with scarlet. My gut tied in knots.
Birds circling.
The sun is bright, burning my strong arms and
dirt caked hands. I squint. My back is tight as I
struggle to stand. Rotting carcasses strewn.

Strawberries everywhere.

No junk mail please

Grab a heavy load and march. Left right left
right. Dump her in the wagon boys! And repeat!

Left right left right.
Wallop. Thump. Wallop ,thump.
The sounds of magazines slapping each other for
space, jousting in the crowded car boot.

Unload boys.
Thwack. Wallop. Thwack and wallop.
Magazines hit the lounge-room floor.
Production line time.
Stack. Fold. Elastic band.
Boys to ATTENTION!

Stack fold elastic band.
TWANG!! Stray elastic band.
THIS MEANS WAR!!!!

Wallop. Thump. Wallop. Thump.
Boys will be boys.

Wallop. Thump. Wallop. Thump.
Mum will bring consequence and balance.

Watch out for that tree

Soaring high
Wingless but birdlike
Towards the sunshine
Swooping, spiralling, hovering.

My tail flapping, wind beneath my wings
Arcs, slow fast and looping.
I feel a pull, a little tug- then stronger-more aggressive
Something has caught me
Down I go, drifting laboriously from side to side
Slow dips lower and lower

Now I'm grounded. Settled on green tarmac. Someone whines and winds beside me. The slack goes taut, I am pulled in close and held tight. We are waiting together.

The wind whistles and whispers and wails through the trees. I imagine my rusty engine rumbling to life. I also imagine swallowing my fish and fluffing my feathers. Instead I soar, at the end of the line, my tail blue and spiraling behind me in the gusty breeze. I am a kite.

And there is a tree. Now I am trapped. The wrong kind of high. Sore not soar. I feel winding. I hear whining. But alas I am well stuck.

“Watch out for that TREE!”

The local

Our local, a hop skip and triple jump away from home. If one has longish legs.

Mum's occasional secret late night chocolate fix, never occasional, always often and not ever a secret.
The teen needs a Pringles can, for what you ask…so do I.
Curly Wurly woo time for the daughter, crazy loopy caramel for a loopy lil cutie.

No toy. No toy. Put it back. Put it down. Where did you get that from. This isn't good behaviour. No treat for you. Stomp. Huff. Tears pending. Negotiations imminent always. Put that back. Put that away. Don't touch. Look with your eyes. No hands. See this toy inside chocolate. A kinder? A yowie?
Eat first then you may… yes you may; that means JUST THIS ONCE.

Holdup! How many times has just this once happened? Huff. Stomp. Mum is cranky. Quick let's go back for more chocolate.

Queasy

Car trip. YEW!
Dunno where we are going...
Eat a Quell or five . Dabble in some ginger potion too.
BUT...are we there yet?
Winding roads, car rolling and lurching like a old vessel on the tarmac turns.
Belly rolling and turning in sync.
Mum's an ace at the wheel. She rides the waves like a sailor, the ups, the downs, the lulls in the eye of the storm.
Hill. Look let's go; UP UP UP! Butterflies climbing like abseil ropes on a cliff.
And race DOWN. DOWN. DOWN.
Belly dropping through the floor at the valley base and lungs clawing into the throat.
Tumble drier or stomach? Churning in the sud.
UP.UP. UP

And....OUT.OUT.OUT.
Plastering the car faster than a professional gyprocker.
Windows DOWN. DOWN.DOWN.

Sheep for sleep

Not tired.
Not sleepy.
I am wide awake.

Counting sheep one...two...three
Forty seven...forty eight...
That is a lot of sheep! Someone needs to keep them in check.

Counting sheepdoggies... Ratio has got to be right...
One ...two...

I wonder how many ticks they would all have?
One..two.......
thirty five...thirty six... thirty seven

How many houses would they need if ticks had houses? Backpacker style or B & B, hotel maybe...
One...two... three...
ARGGHHHhhhh!!!

The roof is caving in on this B & B and I swear I have fur up my left nostril.... RUN RUN RUN,

Scratch scratch scratch.
Once, twice, thrice....
ZZZZzzzzzzzz

Anaphylactic

No Egg. No nuts. No pets.

Sure fine, no worries, okay.

No pavlova at Christmas, no bacon carbonara, no mudcake....

Sure thing mum!

No patting dogs, no petting rabbits, no feather doonas, no wool jumpers, no sheepskin Ugg's...

Sure thing mum!

No snickers Betty, no cinema trips, no peanut brittle, no Nutella, no mango macadamia ice-cream, no coconut body butter, no nourishing shampoos, no box of favourites or roses, no satay, no Chinese takeaway, no korma.

Sure thing mum!

No standing near me when I eat peanut butter, no hugging if I've used coco body tan, I have washed my hair in hazel shampoo, I patted the neighbour's dog ..So...

STAND CLEAR

No sleepovers. No school camps. No trick or treating.
No school prize box. No pizza nights. No life.

Hey mum?
Stab me with that pen?
The Epi-pen.
Please.
Maybe then I'll feel alive.

The box

Zombies walking. To the box and back.
Zombies.
Eating; to the fridge and back.
Zombies saying yes. What was said no-one knows.
Zombies brushing teeth.
The mirror shows glazed eyes and drool.
Knock knock; anyone home?
No answer.

Candles

Why I need a cake.
Because:
Sprinkles and icing and sugar rush wheeeeee!
Fluffy sponge and chocolate mud without a shower required.
The calories don't count today right?
Edible flowers and cake toppers and nude buttercream and the perfect drip,
Or cupcakes, more to share or really more for mwah.
I choose oreo, pretzel, vanilla, pb & j, orange poppy, carrot walnut, while chocolate,
I don't choose; I have one of each, snaffle snaffle, lick lick.
Delirious I giggle.
Manic but sated I'm suddenly hit, the sugar crashs claims me, then slumber too.
This party seems to be over....

Tradie boy

Noticed your guarded smile.
And definitely NOT your legs!
Noticed your can do attitude.
And definitely not your eclectic threads.
Noticed your perchant for veg.
And definitely not your dreads!

Something about watching a man work hard,
Sweltering under the harsh summer sun,
Makes a woman feel things,
She wishes could just be done.

But alas and a lack.
Misunderstood!
Friendship or good company or silence in
solitude or a place to call home.

Many strings to our bows we each have.
And the beats play seperate songs, a divided riff
on the same album. So keep tapping that,
keeping the rhythm, keeping in time; as we beat
along to the rhythm of life. Parallel.

Teens

A yell and a slam, A swear word with ma'am, or mother or some such thing,
To rude and too crude to note, yet dwell on it I will. Not the words as such, but the harsh tone, the sweaty upper lip, the door jam impaled in the wall.

What could it possibly be? To make him seeth, with such a ferocious aggressive abandon,
Surely not this new world, full of genders galore, where every step to take is wrong, and your mother's a whore...

Imagine me this- teen years of bliss, climbing trees, skipping stones, riding bikes, getting loans; toys from a mate, maybe a watch too, the latest go kart, a skiff with a view. Where did we go wrong, now a good time is tech and a bong.

Please bring back my teen to the trees, the birds and the bees, and not this fowl that keeps following me around, clucking and pecking and ruffling and cursing.
Bring the sunshine back. Bring my teen out of his shell, away from the smell of dope in the

shed and cable in the bed. Bring him back to his life, in good health and not strife. Bring him back home, where good habits are sown, and just like the seed from loins he once was he can flourish and grow, no more to be said mum is a hoe.

Amen to that.

www.ingramcontent.com/pod-product-compliance
Lightning Source LLC
Chambersburg PA
CBHW062205160726
48282CB00027B/1001
* 9 7 8 9 3 5 7 6 9 6 5 6 2 *